# AWAITED

# AWAITED

## *An Advent Devotional for Catholic Couples*

CARISSA PLUTA AND
STEPHANIE CALIS

Published by Spoken Bride

# Copyright

+ AMDG +

Written and Edited by Carissa Pluta and Stephanie Calis
Cover Art and Layout by Andi Compton
Cover Photo by Styled Stock House

Published by Spoken Bride, a ministry for Catholic brides and newlyweds

www.spokenbride.com

# Contents

# Introduction

Do you remember a time in your life as a couple––perhaps during your engagement or perhaps as you neared the end of an extended time apart––when you each experienced a deep sense of longing for the other? Do you remember the feelings of excitement, joy, and awe as you counted down the days until that awaited moment?

Do you remember the moment your desires were brought to fruition?

Of course, while beauty exists in the fulfillment of your excitement, beauty also exists in the waiting.

You wouldn't roll up to your wedding without any plans. You took time to find the perfect dress, plan the menu, pick colors and flowers. You talked to your priest, signed up for marriage prep classes, sent save-the-dates to your loved ones.

Nor would you forget about the coming of your beloved. You cleaned the house and made the bed. You cooked a meal and set the table. You readied your space and yourself, wanting to ensure that your spouse felt known and loved upon arrival.

The season of preparation purifies your heart and your desires, making you ever more ready to receive the gift of the other.

In this new liturgical season, we as a church remember the coming of Christ ––both on Christmas day and at the end of time––and we intentionally work on readying ourselves to receive him when that blessed moment finally comes.

This book was written to guide you in truly welcoming the Christ Child, the long-awaited King of your souls, in a daily-reflection format. For each of the four weeks of Advent, you'll find a particular focus:

- Week 1: Preparing your home
- Week 2: Preparing your family
- Week 3: Preparing your marriage
- Week 4: Preparing your hearts

Each week, you will spend time with the Word of God, letting Him speak to you through the words of the Old and the New Testament. You will read and reflect on unique virtues to build up during this season, and tangible ways to cultivate them in your life. And finally, you'll encounter various forms of prayer that will help you delve deeper into these themes and that you can return to even after the season has ended.

Take some time each day to pray through this book together as a couple. We pray that each page will draw you deeper into conversation with one another and with God.

You may notice that this book is not tied to any particular Advent season (as specific dates, daily mass readings, and the like are not included) so these prayers and reflections can continue to serve you and your spouse, year after year.

Embrace this season, embrace the longing and anticipation it brings. Remember His promise to complete your joy. Wait in hope. The Awaited One––He who will transform our marriages and our lives ––is near.

# Week 1: Preparing Your Home

Advent stands out among the liturgical seasons as a marvelously sensual season in which the Church pulls out all of the "smells and bells" to celebrate. Through the candles, the incense, the hymns present in our places of worship, we tangibly experience the sacred beauty of our Creator, and our internal dispositions turn heavenward in response to the encounter. These items are more than just outward signs; they help us to more fully enter into the mystery of the Incarnation.

The physical world isn't accidental or inconsequential in the plan of God. It was designed with us in mind and redeemed by Christ when He lovingly stepped into it. The Almighty God taking on human flesh shows us that even in this messy world, God can--and in fact, does--dwell. He meets us where we live.

In the vocation of marriage, your home, your Domestic Church, is the primary place where you find God in your day-to-day life. In it, you will hear the constant, and often challenging, call to love. In it your heart will stretch and grow and flourish. If you want to truly meet

Christ, you must first work on building your home into a place of encounter.

In this first week of Advent, we will dive into the biblical and personal significance of home, as well as ways to cultivate your space to more fully enter into the spirit of this season. (No, we aren't just talking about Advent Wreaths, though if you have one, now is definitely the time to dust it off).

In the same way, God made Himself known to the world in the small stable in Bethlehem, He wants to reveal Himself to you and your spouse in your home. Open your doors and hearts to Him today.

**Discuss:** *How have you prepared your homes in the past? Did you find that helped or hindered your internal preparation for the coming of Christ? What might you want to do differently this year?*

# A Place of Encounter

**Read: Exodus 40:18-19, 34-38**

*It was Moses who set up the tabernacle. He placed its pedestals, set up its frames, put in its bars, and set up its columns.*

*He spread the tent over the tabernacle and put the covering on top of the tent, as the LORD had commanded him.*

*Then the cloud covered the tent of meeting, and the glory of the LORD filled the tabernacle.*

*Moses could not enter the tent of meeting, because the cloud settled down upon it and the glory of the LORD filled the tabernacle.*

*Whenever the cloud rose from the tabernacle, the Israelites would set out on their journey.*

*But if the cloud did not lift, they would not go forward; only when it lifted did they go forward.*

*The cloud of the LORD was over the tabernacle by day, and fire in the cloud at night, in the sight of the whole house of Israel in all the stages of their journey.*

**Reflect:**

In the Book of Exodus, God commanded Moses to build the Ark of the Lord, or a tabernacle to house the pot of manna, Aaron's rod, and the stone tablets containing the Ten Commandments––symbols of God's covenant with the Israelites. Several chapters are dedicated solely to the process of building the tabernacle and detailing its characteristics as given by the Lord in Exodus chapters 25-31.

The tent of meeting, where the Ark resided, was a holy place where God would meet His people. And this place of encounter was portable, so it accompanied the Israelites on their journey through the wilderness.

How mysterious and tender it is, that God would descend from on high into the hiddenness of the sanctuary created by the hands of men. The Almighty God certainly didn't need a physical dwelling place in order to speak to us. But, because He is the loving Father he is, He put our needs first and came to meet us where we are.

And, not only did He deem it worthy to enter into our world, God took care of each little detail. He took time to explain (down to the exact measurements!) the features of his dwelling, and He entrusted man with the creation of it. And He does the same for us.

God entrusts couples with the responsibility of creating a home that resembles a tabernacle, that foreshadows the communion of heaven and the fulfillment of God's covenant with his people. And He can inspire and direct you as husband and wife in the building of it.

God wants to accompany you on your journey to the heavenly

promised land, as well. In the vocation of marriage, so much of your journey will take place in your home, where you live your shared life. You wake up in the morning and go to sleep at night under your roof; you share laughter and meals around your table and form memories that will last. Your four walls will hold many, if not all, of your marriage's joys and sorrows.

Your Christian home, then, takes on the quality of a tabernacle, it foreshadows the communion of heaven, the fulfillment of God's covenant with his people.

He wants to meet you right where you are; He wants to create a space for Himself in your midst. Will you help Him?

**Act:**
This Advent we are called into moments of prayer and reflection. Between work schedules, kids' activities or schoolwork, or the festivities that accompany this time of year most of us won't have time to spend these moments in the chapel every day. But we can meet God everyday in our homes, if only we can find ways to recognize His presence.

Where will you spend time in prayer during this season? You don't need an elaborate prayer corner; maybe you can place a small statue on your nightstand, or a candle on the coffee table. Talk as a couple about dedicating space in your home to pray (and read through this devotional), even if only for the next few weeks. Create space in your home to encounter Christ.

In the tent of meeting, Moses arranged bread on the tables. He lit lamps and burned incense, actions that remind us of the preparation of the altar during Mass. Moses, through God's direction, created a sacred space which invited man's participation. God wants us to actively engage with Him in our domestic churches.

Our sacred space should reflect this. Don't make it a place you can't touch. Light candles, set up a holy water font, leave a journal there with your prayer intentions. Make it a central place in your home and come to it often.

# The Spirit of Home

**Read:** Luke 1:26-38

*In the sixth month, the angel Gabriel was sent from God to a town of
Galilee called Nazareth,*

*to a virgin betrothed to a man named Joseph, of the house of David, and
the virgin's name was Mary.*

*And coming to her, he said, "Hail, favored one! The Lord is with you."*

*But she was greatly troubled at what was said and pondered what sort of
greeting this might be.*

*Then the angel said to her, "Do not be afraid, Mary, for you have found
favor with God.*

*Behold, you will conceive in your womb and bear a son, and you shall
name him Jesus.*

*He will be great and will be called Son of the Most High,\* and the Lord
God will give him the throne of David his father,*

*and he will rule over the house of Jacob forever, and of his kingdom there will be no end."*

*But Mary said to the angel, "How can this be, since I have no relations with a man?"*

*And the angel said to her in reply, "The holy Spirit will come upon you, and the power of the Most High will overshadow you. Therefore the child to be born will be called holy, the Son of God.*

*And behold, Elizabeth, your relative, has also conceived\* a son in her old age, and this is the sixth month for her who was called barren;*

*for nothing will be impossible for God."*

*Mary said, "Behold, I am the handmaid of the Lord. May it be done to me according to your word." Then the angel departed from her.*

**Reflect:**

The Litany of Loreto refers to Mary as the Ark of the New Covenant. In comparing yesterday's reading from Exodus with today's passage from Luke, we can see a clear connection. We observe a lot of similarities in the imagery and wording of the two passages: A cloud overshadowed the tent and the glory of the filled the tabernacle. The angel told Mary that the Holy Spirit would overshadow her and she would conceive Jesus, the Glory of God.

As we dig deeper, we can uncover more parallels. The tabernacle described in Exodus contained signs of God's covenant with Israel but these signs also prefigure God's eternal covenant with man established through Jesus: the Ten Commandments, the law of God and Jesus who will fulfill the law. Aaron's rod was the symbol of Aaron's priesthood, and Jesus is the true high priest. And of course, the manna or the bread that came down from heaven heralds the Eucharist.

Mary held within her womb the New Covenant. Her body became a physical place for Christ to dwell before His birth. She is a temple, a tabernacle, a worthy home for the Savior. Through her, God found Himself a home in human nature. The Ark and the tabernacles in our churches are mere shadows of the first home of the God-made-man. And if our home is a shadow of the tabernacle, then it is also a shadow of the Blessed Mother.

Mary's humility and simplicity made her the most perfect, most hospitable dwelling for the Lord.

She opened both her heart and her body to receive Him in however he wished to come to her. Through her words and deeds, she pointed only toward God.

While tangible pieces of our home invite us to go deeper in our relationship to God, and while we should cultivate beauty in our dwelling place, our homes do not have to look like they came straight from an influencer's Instagram feed. We don't have to achieve a certain aesthetic in our homes for them to be worthy of God's presence.

Our homes can reflect the truth about God, both in tangible ways like creating a sacred space or displaying our Advent wreath, and in intangible ways like cultivating a spirit of hospitality and peace. We want our homes, like Mary, to communicate Beauty Himself to those who live there--and those who don't.

**Act:**
The Blessed Mother became a worthy dwelling for Christ because of her virtue. In Saint Louis de Montfort's *True Devotion to Mary*, he lists the ten principal virtues of Mary:

- Profound humility
- Lively faith
- Blind obedience
- Continual prayer
- Universal mortification
- Divine purity
- Ardent charity
- Heroic patience
- Angelic sweetness
- Divine wisdom

Which virtues do you recognize as a part of your home life? Which virtues does your home life lack? Pray with these virtues and ask the Holy Spirit for guidance. Discuss with your spouse how you can continue to foster a Mary-like spirit within your dwelling place. Pick one of these virtues and decide on a practical way to practice that virtue this week.

# Simplicity

When you imagine the birth of the Savior, what do your senses experience?

No decorations, no gaggle of loved ones, no scents of pine or baking. And yet, in the humble stable of Christ's birth, there was light. There were the bonds of love between Our Lady and Saint Joseph, filled with awe even amid the uncertainty of the next steps in their journey. There were the sounds of heavenly glory--a literal choir of angels.

It's hard to imagine a more sacramental event than the Incarnation: a material reality of immaterial, divine love come down to us in human form. Have you ever considered that the material preparation of your home in this season has significant potential for the same?

Christ's birth was humble, poor, and hidden. The adornments of the season invite you into the paradox of the Incarnation: what initially appears so simple is, in reality, so endlessly wondrous and mysterious.

How will you make this paradox visible in your home this season? All of the material, external adornments you choose to engage with during Advent--a Christmas tree, lighting, Nativity set, music, meals, and more--invite us to contemplate beauty in a sensory way. These trim-mings hold so much meaning when viewed in light of the deeper beauty at work: the Father's gift of himself to us on that first quiet night in Bethlehem.

And yet, in light of this week's preparation of your home, and the essential point that a tabernacle is sacred *simply because the Lord is present*, it's worth considering the ultimate purpose of any adornments we choose for our homes. You might feel tempted to fill your Advent with stuff: how many things on our to-do lists do we still need to prepare? How many parties and events are on the calendar? How many devotions are we taking up?

However, you find simplicity by chipping away at the unnecessary parts of something to more fully reveal its essence. Enter into the tension of adornment and sensory goods as they relate to inviting the Lord's presence in your home, in whatever way that looks like for you as a couple.

**Act:**
No matter what your budget, living situation, and preferred traditions, take time today to talk with each other about the décor and celebrations you hope to bring into your home in this season, and how they might consistently draw your attention to the simplicity of the Nativity: Is it through waiting until late in Advent (or even Christmas Eve) to hang ornaments or listen to Christmas hymns? Through religious art or sculpture that you'll reserve for displaying only at this time of year? Through daily acts of sacrifice for the duration of Advent?

No answers are wrong! Enter into this Advent season with a spirit of quiet simplicity, seeking to reveal and invite Him over seeking greater quantities of preparations, and watch how it amplifies into a resounding joy at Christmas.

# Hospitality

Worship musicians Harvest Bashta sing,

*Let there be oil in my lamp,*
*Let the fire not go out,*
*When I hear the Bridegroom come.*

This song, "Make Us Ready," nods to the Parable of the Ten Virgins in Matthew's Gospel. You can easily see the significance of this reference in the Advent season, as well. This first week of preparation invites us to ready ourselves for Christ's coming, cultivating a spirit of light, anticipation, and attention.

When you think of holiday hospitality, parties and gatherings often come to mind, and rightly so. Opening your doors to friends and family offers opportunities to bear Christ to one another in every encounter. He who is all goodness, beauty, truth, and mercy is present when we gather in His name. Challenge yourself today to think on the meaning of hospitality to Christ, himself: how will you prepare--how will you make yourselves ready--to welcome His presence into your home?

Lighting the lamps, building the fire, and setting the table are all ways we prepare to open our door to guests. Opening the doors of our homes and gathering at the table are intimate expressions of relationship and community. And hospitality is figurative, not just literal, when we open ourselves and our homes to spiritual transformation. Will we be ready? Will we embrace the Savior's coming?

Christ, the Bridegroom, approaches and knocks. Let us prepare a home for Him.

**Act:**

Listen to the song cited above. Pray specifically for a spirit of hospitality and a readiness to embrace Christ's movements within our hearts. Ask the Lord to draw your attention, as a couple, to the areas in which he desires our presence.

# Silence

*"And Mary kept all these things, reflecting on them in her heart."* (Luke 2:19).

Anyone else read this account of the Nativity from Luke's Gospel, wish to imitate Our Lady in quiet reflection, and...fail?

It sounds beyond obvious to state that Advent is a season for quiet; for silence. Yet putting it into practice can be challenging with Christmas music, sales, social gatherings, and the ever-present call of our phones.

In response, you might feel tempted toward extremes: hard restrictions on listening and phone habits, spending, socializing. And those practices can prove effective! Consider, though, how an excess of restrictions can quickly feel, well, *restrictive*. Healthy boundaries encourage freedom to choose the most fulfilling good for your situation--not a sense of enslavement to rules.

If you've experienced this sense of pressure, to make your Advent the *most* reflective, the *most* silent, the *most* significant, try a balanced approach. What if, instead of heavily restricting your habits in favor of silence, you just tried a day, or even an hour, at a time? As you spend this week focusing on the preparation of your home as a dwelling for the Lord, identify ways to find refuge and quiet within the walls of your own dwelling place.

For you, this might look like reading Scripture or praying the Joyful Mysteries of the Rosary as you make coffee and prepare for your day. It might look like a weekly holy hour before the Blessed Sacrament, or an evening routine that facilitates conversation and reconnection with your beloved.

Practicing silence in small, meaningful intervals can bring surprising order and peace to the rhythms of your days, apart and together. After all, the silence of the Bethlehem stable was--quite literally--life-giving.

**Act:**
Sit on the couch with your fiancé or spouse for a period of silence and retreat from distractions, with the expectation that it's just for tonight. Leave your phones in another room, turn off music and TV, and use the time to talk, pray silently or together, or to read from the Scriptures or a spiritual book.

And if you find this time fruitful, take up the challenge of making it a weekly event.

# And the Word Became Flesh and Dwelt Among Us

"The Word became flesh and dwelt among us."

During this first week of Advent, we meditated on the truth of an Omnipotent God taking on our human flesh and entering into a physical dwelling in our world. The Greek word for dwell (*skenoo*) used in John 1:14, can be literally translated "to pitch a tent."

We've reflected on the ways He has (and continues) to make Himself known in the world, discussed the need for making our own dwelling a peaceful and life-giving place, and began the work of intentionally cultivating it.

As we close out the first week of our journey, we'd like to introduce (or perhaps, re-introduce) you to a unique form of praying with Scripture, called *Lectio Divina*.

This ancient Catholic practice of *Lectio Divina* (Latin for "Divine Reading") immerses you in the Word of God and helps you listen more closely to what the Lord wants you to hear. It works particularly well with the Gospels, but you can use it with any passage to gain deeper and more personal insight into the Scriptures. You can find suggestions for other passages to use for further mediation in the Appendix.

Today we will pray with this passage from the Gospel of John that highlights the mystery and beauty of God entering the world; his "pitching His tent" among us. Let us open our hearts and minds to the still, small voice inviting us to a deeper relationship with Him.

*Come Holy Spirit.*

## HOW TO PRAY LECTIO DIVINA

**Lectio:** Begin with a slow, prayerful, deliberate reading (and then re-reading) of a Scripture passage. Together with your spouse, take turns reading the passage below out loud.

**Meditatio:** Spend time meditating on the passage, with the Holy Spirit as your guide. What word or phrase stuck out to you during the reading? What does this word/phrase mean? How does this relate to your prayer from this first week of Advent?

**Oratio:** Invite God into conversation. Ask Him what He wants you to learn from the passage. Ask God to reveal why that particular word or phrase stuck out and what He desires you to learn from it.

**Contemplatio:** Spend time to rest in silence and dwell in the presence of God. Allow what has been stirred up in your souls during the previous steps to take root.

**Operatio:** You should never walk away from an encounter with the Lord unchanged. Discuss your prayer with your spouse and create an action plan based on your conversation with God: What is the next step in this area of your life? What practical resolutions can you commit to, and how can you incorporate it into your life?

### JOHN 1: 1-18

In the beginning was the Word,

and the Word was with God,

and the Word was God.

He was in the beginning with God.

All things came to be through him,

and without him nothing came to be.

What came to be

through him was life,

and this life was the light of the human race;

the light shines in the darkness,

and the darkness has not overcome it.

A man named John was sent from God.

He came for testimony, to testify to the light, so that all might believe through him.

He was not the light, but came to testify to the light.

The true light, which enlightens everyone, was coming into the world.

He was in the world,

and the world came to be through him,

but the world did not know him.

He came to what was his own,

but his own people did not accept him.

But to those who did accept him he gave power to become children of God, to those who believe in his name,

who were born not by natural generation nor by human choice nor by a man's decision but of God.

And the Word became flesh

and made his dwelling among us,

and we saw his glory,

the glory as of the Father's only Son,

full of grace and truth.

John testified to him and cried out, saying, "This was he of whom I said, 'The one who is coming after me ranks ahead of me because he existed before me.'"

From his fullness we have all received, grace in place of grace, because while the law was given through Moses, grace and truth came through Jesus Christ.

No one has ever seen God. The only Son, God, who is at the Father's side, has revealed him.

# Week 2: Preparing Your Family

At the heart of the divine mystery of the Incarnation, we find a family. Incredibly, the Creator of the world, almighty and eternal, entered human history in just the same way we do: by sharing in family life.

Last week we discussed the importance of the physical space you inhabit as a couple. But even more meaningful than the tangible aspects of your home is the culture you create together, as a family within that space.

The unique culture in your home--traditions, habits, practices, and values--defines your identity as a family whether you have children or not. It leads to moments of true encounter and meaningful connection. As husband and wife, you take on responsibility for building up and living out this culture to the enrichment of other member(s) and to strengthen the bonds between you.

As Christians, as sons and daughters of God, we have a rich family heritage and history that deserves to be remembered and celebrated--in the ways we pray together, work together, and live together, especially within Advent.

During this second week of Advent, we will examine the theme of family throughout Salvation History by reading key biblical passages, and discuss the meaningful ways in which we can build up our family during this liturgical season, actively growing the family of God.

**Discuss:** *What makes our family unique? What do we value? Do we live our life with these values in mind?*

# The Weight of a Covenant

**Read: Genesis 22: 1-18**

*Some time afterward, God put Abraham to the test and said to him: Abraham! "Here I am!" he replied.*

*Then God said: Take your son Isaac, your only one, whom you love, and go to the land of Moriah. There offer him up as a burnt offering on one of the heights that I will point out to you.*

*Early the next morning Abraham saddled his donkey, took with him two of his servants and his son Isaac, and after cutting the wood for the burnt offering, set out for the place of which God had told him.*

*On the third day Abraham caught sight of the place from a distance.*

*Abraham said to his servants: "Stay here with the donkey, while the boy and I go on over there. We will worship and then come back to you."*

*So Abraham took the wood for the burnt offering and laid it on his son Isaac, while he himself carried the fire and the knife. As the two walked on together,*

Isaac spoke to his father Abraham. "Father!" he said. "Here I am," he replied. Isaac continued, "Here are the fire and the wood, but where is the sheep for the burnt offering?"

"My son," Abraham answered, "God will provide the sheep for the burnt offering." Then the two walked on together.

When they came to the place of which God had told him, Abraham built an altar there and arranged the wood on it. Next he bound his son Isaac, and put him on top of the wood on the altar.

Then Abraham reached out and took the knife to slaughter his son.

But the angel of the LORD called to him from heaven, "Abraham, Abraham!" "Here I am," he answered.

"Do not lay your hand on the boy," said the angel. "Do not do the least thing to him. For now I know that you fear God, since you did not withhold from me your son, your only one."

Abraham looked up and saw a single ram caught by its horns in the thicket. So Abraham went and took the ram and offered it up as a burnt offering in place of his son.

Abraham named that place Yahweh-yireh; hence people today say, "On the mountain the LORD will provide."

A second time the angel of the LORD called to Abraham from heaven

and said: "I swear by my very self—oracle of the LORD—that because you acted as you did in not withholding from me your son, your only one,

I will bless you and make your descendants as countless as the stars of the *sky and the sands of the seashore; your descendants will take possession of the gates of their enemies,*

*and in your descendants all the nations of the earth will find blessing, because you obeyed my command."*

### Reflect:

Genesis Chapter 22 finds Abraham ascending a mountain, prepared to offer *his only son* in obedience and sacrifice. What pain must have pierced him as he brought Isaac to the altar. What doubts might have echoed in his heart.

And yet, father and son ascend the altar, ready to entrust themselves to the Lord. John Bergsma in *Bible Basics for Catholics* writes: "Isaac and Abraham walk quietly up Mount Mariah and stand before God to make their reply: 'We are.' We can see why God is so moved by their willingness--so moved that he does something for Abraham that he has only done for a handful of people in all of human history: he swears an oath to him."(1)

The Lord promises Abraham blessing and promises innumerable descendants. A covenant. "Throughout the Bible, 'swearing an oath' and 'making a covenant' mean almost the same thing, somewhat like 'exchanging vows' and 'getting married' are almost synonymous."(2) Generations later, of course, we see in Jesus Christ another ascent up a hill. Another perfect act of obedience and sacrificial love; this time, one that opens wide the doors to eternal life.

In marriage, God calls spouses to the same self-emptying love, to the point of laying their own pain upon an altar. A vow--*we are*--a covenant, unbreakable and encompassing all our bleeding wounds, trusting we'll be loved all the same.

**Act:**

Take time today to reflect on the fulfillment of God's covenant found in the Nativity, and the weight of your own wedding vows. What parts of you and your beloved is He drawing into the light--even the parts we're inclined to hide--ready to bring to new life?

Moreover, what will the blessing and descendants of your own vocation be like? What will be your legacy? Talk with your fiancé or spouse about concrete ways to embody and pass on your faith to others--whether through biological descendants, through service to the Church, and otherwise.

(1) Cf. John Bergsma, *Bible Basics for Catholics*. Ave Maria Press, 2012.
(2) Ibid.

# What Has Brought You to This Moment?

**Read: Matthew 1: 1-17**
*The book of the genealogy of Jesus Christ, the son of David, the son of Abraham.*

*Abraham became the father of Isaac, Isaac the father of Jacob, Jacob the father of Judah and his brothers.*

*Judah became the father of Perez and Zerah, whose mother was Tamar.d Perez became the father of Hezron, Hezron the father of Ram,*

*Ram the father of Amminadab. Amminadab became the father of Nahshon, Nahshon the father of Salmon,*

*Salmon the father of Boaz, whose mother was Rahab. Boaz became the father of Obed, whose mother was Ruth. Obed became the father of Jesse,*

*Jesse the father of David the king.*

*David became the father of Solomon, whose mother had been the wife of Uriah.*

*Solomon became the father of Rehoboam, Rehoboam the father of Abijah, Abijah the father of Asaph.*

*Asaph became the father of Jehoshaphat, Jehoshaphat the father of Joram, Joram the father of Uzziah.*

*Uzziah became the father of Jotham, Jotham the father of Ahaz, Ahaz the father of Hezekiah. Hezekiah became the father of Manasseh, Manasseh the father of Amos, Amos the father of Josiah.*

*Josiah became the father of Jechoniah and his brothers at the time of the Babylonian exile.*

*After the Babylonian exile, Jechoniah became the father of Shealtiel, Shealtiel the father of Zerubbabel,*

*Zerubbabel the father of Abiud. Abiud became the father of Eliakim, Eliakim the father of Azor,*
*Azor the father of Zadok. Zadok became the father of Achim, Achim the father of Eliud,*

*Eliud the father of Eleazar. Eleazar became the father of Matthan, Matthan the father of Jacob,*

*Jacob the father of Joseph, the husband of Mary. Of her was born Jesus who is called the Messiah.*

*Thus the total number of generations from Abraham to David is fourteen generations; from David to the Babylonian exile, fourteen generations; from the Babylonian exile to the Messiah, fourteen generations.*

**Reflect:**

Yesterday, you reflected on God's covenant with Abraham; His promise of descendants, a legacy, and a future. Today, you'll read the genealogy of Abraham that shows the Father's faithfulness to that covenant. Jesus fulfills God's promise; generation by generation, we see the necessity of *family* in His plan for our salvation.

Matthew's Gospel begins with a genealogy: over a dozen generations, beginning with Abraham, that ultimately lead to Joseph's betrothal to Mary. And, through Mary and the Holy Spirit, the begetting of Jesus. This is a family.

What about your own family genealogy? In marriage, you and your spouse form a new family, one that establishes its own distinct beginning for generations to come--whether that beginning resounds in your own children and grandchildren, or through spiritual parenthood and the lasting legacy of your witness.

It's profound to consider the genetic odds of you and your spouse existing exactly as you are: the necessity of your ancestors being exactly who *they* were; the unbrokenness of your family lines; the exact timing and biological makeup of your conception. The chances of you each existing, just as you are, are literally one among millions. To consider that within those chances you have found one another, and are called to marriage, is nothing short of cosmic. Divine. Entirely intentional.

Perhaps this Advent season finds you and your beloved preparing for increased time with family. What will this experience be like for each of you? Even with the knowledge that family is eternal and that grace has led you from your families of origin toward the new family formed by your marriage vows, it's normal to feel the ache of division, brokenness, and loss within your respective families. Confronting family wounds and conflicts is painful, and will never be without flaw during our earthly lives.

Enter into whatever pain you feel, and spend time talking today about concrete, practical ways to recognize conflicts within your families of origin and maintain suitable boundaries around your relationship. As spouses--as your own family--how can you shield and support one another while maintaining an appropriate level of respect toward in-laws?

Christ's own lineage included sin, mistrust, and broken relationships. Meditate on the idea that He truly truly does make all things new, and desires to be present in your family. Amid any family challenges in this season, invite Him in during these days of preparation. He has brought you both here, exactly as you are. As with Abraham, Jesus comes to fulfill our families.

**Act:**

Take a moment to reflect silently on the idea that each of your families' past generations and relationships, whatever their imperfections, have brought you both here to your specific love and specific vocation. Ask Christ to enter into your families and into your relationship.

Pray, *we entrust our family to you.* What habits from your families of origin do you hope to carry into your marriage, and which do you hope to amend and rewrite?

# Traditions

Jesus's own family history, as told in the Scripture reflections from the past two days, gives context and meaning to the magnitude of God's entering into human history. We, the Body of Christ, are connected by the bonds of the universal Church and the sacraments, and look to the traditions of the Church to ground and unite us.

In the same way, every earthly family finds identity and belonging in a variety of connections and traditions--especially during this time of year.

There is such anticipation and joy in the sharing of your childhood holiday traditions with your spouse, combining your family rituals into something new and distinctive.

When you think about your favorite traditions for Advent and Christmas, what comes to mind? Moreover, *when* and *how* did these traditions take root? Maybe you can't remember a time before your family put up the tree on a certain date, attended an annual event, or did your gift exchange in a particular way. Alternatively, maybe a specific recipe, song, or movie didn't become firmly established in your rituals until later on; perhaps a seemingly insignificant selection took on greater meaning and grew into a tradition over time.

You might feel ready to dive headlong into this time, eager to introduce every one of your cherished traditions to your beloved and enjoy them as a couple. And that desire is good! But what if overwhelm creeps in, or traditions feel like an obligation?

It's alright, and good, to be intentional about what traditions you and your spouse hope to continue--or not--as you form a new family. Consider this an invitation to decide, together, that the holiday rituals from your families of origin can continue, evolve, or even fade away as you enter into your life together. Creating updated or original traditions of your own can become one of the most precious parts of each holiday you spend as husband and wife!

And what if your past includes more painful holiday memories than good ones? If one or both of you comes from difficult family situations, acknowledge your pain while placing your hope in Christ. Throughout Advent we await Him, anticipating the hope and restoration brought by His birth.

Embrace the creativity and possibility of your own new traditions, and take time today to talk about the ways you can prepare to meet Him in the manger.

**Act:**
Discuss the family Advent and Christmas traditions you each grew up with. Which of these traditions do you hope to continue in your marriage?

Are there other traditions you'd like to adopt as a couple? Brainstorm and dream together. You might consider the following traditions:

- What sacred items would we like to have in our home (Advent wreath, Nativity set, etc.)?

- Would we like to acknowledge the liturgical year? Liturgical living possibilities include celebrating feasts of the Church that fall during Advent, like those of Saint Nicholas (December 6), the Immaculate Conception (December 8), Our Lady of Guadalupe (December 12), and Saint Lucy (December 13); waiting until Christmas to place the Christ Child in a nativity set; listening only to secular holiday music during Advent and reserving hymns for the Christmas season.

- How can our prayer in this season increase our anticipation of Christ's coming? Advent prayer possibilities include the Saint Andrew Novena, which traditionally begins on Saint Andrew's feast day (November 30) and is prayed through Christmas Eve, and the O Antiphons, prayed as a part of the Divine Office beginning on December 17 and concluding on Christmas Eve.

- What forms of hospitality and service do we feel called to (hosting a dinner or party for friends, volunteering in a community or parish holiday initiative, making a charitable donation)?

- Would we like to designate a specific date or weekend for tasks like putting up our Christmas tree, decorating our home, or wrapping gifts?

- What recipes, music, literature, and films do we love and want to reserve for this time of year?

# Generosity

As you spend this week preparing your family for the birth of Jesus, consider the many meanings of giving--and its accompaniment, generosity--during the Advent season.

Giving a gift isn't terribly hard--ask anyone who's brought something hilarious or weird to a White Elephant exchange with cousins. But giving with a true spirit of generosity, and considering generosity beyond the material? *So. Much. Harder.*

The Nativity invites us into an encounter: a heavenly Father whose love is so profoundly generous it takes on flesh and blood. A love given without reserve, offering the fulfillment that flows from being known and understood. He seeks us and He knows us--even when we'd rather hide.

A generous heart seeks to silence the reservations and the shame, working to resolve them and pursuing true freedom; sincere understanding. A family culture that embodies generosity is one that receives every person with openness and mercy; a pursuit of the Father's own abundant love for each of His children. How can you live out this virtue, particularly in a world of divided opinions and family dynamics that (not unlike Jesus's own, as recounted in Matthew's Gospel account of Jesus's lineage) might hold lingering wounds?

More often, it's comfortable to keep *some* sense of reservation, keep on at least *some* armor, at holiday events and in daily life: at work events, with family members we haven't seen lately, and even with our beloved. Bad habits, sin, and shame have a way of diminishing generosity, encouraging us to withhold ourselves instead.

What more fitting season, then, when the Lord comes to encounter us so humbly, with such purity of love in the face of a child, to take off the armor? To consider ways He is asking you to give more generously of who you are--in prayer, with family and friends, with your spouse.

Challenge yourselves today to be generous with your time, your personality, and your truest hearts. Ask Him to take down your walls and to make you instruments of encounter. May you strive to see a real and honest vision of each person you interact with, and may you enter into knowing and being known as you are.

**Act:**

Take time today to meditate on the meaning of the word *generosity*. Talk with your beloved about the ways generosity comes easily to you, and about the ways you're tempted to withhold or hide parts of yourselves.

What ways can you each reveal and give of yourselves more fully to the other, and how can you look to Jesus's birth as an example? How can you give of yourselves during this season of more frequent social gatherings and conversations with those who might see differently than you?

# Service

As we remember, not only the coming of Jesus as an infant, but our anticipation for him to come again in glory, we have to ask ourselves: *are we ready?*

In Matthew 25 Jesus paints us a picture of the judgement of nations. He says:

*Then the king will say to those on his right, 'Come, you who are blessed by my Father. Inherit the kingdom prepared for you from the foundation of the world.*

*For I was hungry and you gave me food, I was thirsty and you gave me drink, a stranger and you welcomed me,*

*naked and you clothed me, ill and you cared for me, in prison and you visited me.'*

*Then the righteous will answer him and say, 'Lord, when did we see you hungry and feed you, or thirsty and give you drink?*

*When did we see you a stranger and welcome you, or naked and clothe you?*

*When did we see you ill or in prison, and visit you?'*

*And the king will say to them in reply, 'Amen, I say to you, whatever you did for one of these least brothers of mine, you did for me."*

In this parable, Jesus invites us to recognize Him in all those in need, especially the poor and the marginalized. By loving and serving others, especially those who could never repay us, we love and serve God.

Recognizing and responding to the needs of others in your community–– in your workplace, your parish, and your neighborhood––is not only an important part of the Christian life, but a particular duty of the Christian family. The Church explicitly calls families to work for the betterment of society.

In *Familiaris Consortio*, Pope Saint John Paul II writes: "The social role of the family certainly cannot stop short at procreation and education, even if this constitutes its primary and irreplaceable form of expression. [Families] can and should devote themselves to manifold social service activities, especially in favor of the poor..."(3)

As the basic cell of society, the family has a responsibility to build up the common good, to help create a society that recognizes and upholds the dignity of every human person. The fact that the sacrament of marriage is a public sacrament, not a private one, speaks to this fact. Your Best Man and Maid of Honor stand in as official witnesses on behalf of the whole community. Your marriage, and therefore your family, are not just for you but also for the edification of the entire Church and all its members.

The family, as it mirrors the Trinity and being a communion of persons, was made to reach outside of itself and bear fruit even outside the gift of children. That's the beauty of creating an authentic Christian culture in your family– it's not meant to just *stay* between you; it's meant to be shared. It's meant to run wild and change the world.

God poured himself out for humanity by taking on flesh and all that came with it––hunger, thirst, loneliness, pain, and death. In His boundless compassion He meets us in our needs, and offers to fulfill them. Respond to the generosity of God in the gift of the Incarnation by giving of ourselves in the same way He did––in humble service of others.

**Act:**

With the overwhelming spirit of charity present in this season, there are more than enough opportunities to serve others in your community. Spend some time today to do an examination of sorts on the Corporal Works of Mercy (listed below)––In what ways are you practicing these acts of love? In what ways are you failing to live up to this call?

Then, make a list of the gifts you have to offer––both material and immaterial. What needs do you see in your community? How can you use your gifts to help fill those needs? How can you continue to make God incarnate in the hearts of those in your community both during this season and after it has ended?

Make a plan with your family to respond to one or more of the needs in your community before Christmas.

**Corporal Works of Mercy**

1. Feed the hungry
2. Give drink to the thirsty
3. Clothe the naked
4. Give shelter to travelers

5. Visit the sick
6. Visit the imprisoned
7. Bury the dead

(3) Pope John Paul II, "Familiaris Consortio." *The Holy See, 1981,*
*https://www.vatican.va/content/john-paul-ii/en/apost_exhortations/docu-*
*ments/hf_jp-ii_exh_19811122_familiaris-consortio.html*

# Laying in the Manger

We are now halfway through Advent! Throughout this second week of Advent, we reflected on the theme of family and ways to build up your unique family culture in particular ways this season.

Today, in keeping with this week's theme, we will place ourselves in the moment when Mary and Joseph became the Holy Family with Christ's birth at the Nativity using a form of imaginative prayer known as Ignatian Meditation.

Ignatian Meditation comes from the great spiritual master Saint Ignatius of Loyola, who believed that God can speak to us through our imagination just as He speaks to us through our thoughts and memories.

Think about your daydreams. Perhaps you imagine yourself surrounded by a large gaggle of children at Sunday Mass or writing a best-selling book. Or maybe during your engagement you daydreamed about your wedding day or the house you would one day make into a home.

Daydreams can reveal something about our hearts, and even about our relationships with other people. When examined they can tell you more about who you are and the relationship you have with others.

Similarly, Ignatian Meditation is an act of imagination in which you place yourself in a Gospel scene and live through the acts as a player. By imagining the sights, sounds, and smells of a particular scene, you invite the inspirations of the Spirit, offering you insight into who God is.

Before we begin, it is important to mention that this form of prayer does not come naturally to everyone, and that is totally okay! The more you practice, the easier it will become. God will meet you in this moment, so give it a try--you may even surprise yourself.

*Come Holy Spirit.*

### How to pray with Ignatian Meditation
To fully enter into this spiritual exercise, it can help if you and your spouse take turns guiding one another through the mediation.

After you read the passage aloud to your spouse, slowly read the prompts to help your partner envision themselves in the scene. Your job as the leader is not to have the other person imagining the scene as it is written but to facilitate an encounter with the person of Jesus Christ.

As you listen to the passage, close your eyes and let your imagination go. Don't seek any intellectual insights; just stay with the imagery and let Truth reveal Himself. Use your senses to enter into the scene.

If you feel your imagination going a different way than the prompts suggest, don't be afraid to follow it. There is no "right" way to pray with Ignatian meditation; trust the Holy Spirit to inspire your thoughts and lead you where He desires you to go.

Finally, discuss with one another the fruit of your prayer.

**Read: Luke 2: 1, 4-14**

*In those days a decree went out from Caesar Augustus that the whole world should be enrolled.*

*And Joseph too went up from Galilee from the town of Nazareth to Judea, to the city of David that is called Bethlehem, because he was of the house and family of David,*

*to be enrolled with Mary, his betrothed, who was with child.*

*While they were there, the time came for her to have her child,*

*and she gave birth to her firstborn son. She wrapped him in swaddling clothes and laid him in a manger, because there was no room for them in the inn.*

*Now there were shepherds in that region living in the fields and keeping the night watch over their flock.*

*The angel of the Lord appeared to them and the glory of the Lord shone around them, and they were struck with great fear.*

*The angel said to them, "Do not be afraid; for behold, I proclaim to you good news of great joy that will be for all the people.*

*For today in the city of David a savior has been born for you who is Messiah and Lord.*

*And this will be a sign for you: you will find an infant wrapped in swaddling clothes and lying in a manger."*

*And suddenly there was a multitude of the heavenly host with the angel, praising God and saying:*

*"Glory to God in the highest*

*and on earth peace to those on whom his favor rests."*

**Prompts to guide your mediation:**

- Imagine the sights and sounds of the city flooded with people returning home for the enrollment. Are you in the middle of all the action or looking on from the hills outside of town?

- Who are you in the story? Are you Mary or Joseph? One of the shepherds? An outside observer? What are you doing?

- What does the stable look like as you approach it? It's it large or unassuming? Is it made from wood or hewn in rock?

- What do you see inside? What do you smell and hear? Does it feel warm and cozy or messy and chaotic?

- How do you feel as you enter? Are you afraid or full of awe? Do you feel welcome?

- Who speaks to you? How do you respond?

- What does the baby Jesus look like? Does He look like His mother? Is He crying out for His mother or sleeping peacefully?

- How do you feel looking upon Him?

When you've concluded your meditation, speak to Christ about what you experienced.

# Week 3: Preparing Your Marriage

You have finally made it to the beginning of the third week––Gaudete Sunday. If you have an Advent wreath, you'll light the pink candle and you'll want to make sure you compliment your priest on his *rose* vestments after Mass.

Gaudete Sunday marks the midpoint of Advent, as well as a shift in tone. A penitential feeling pervades the first two weeks of the season, as you acknowledge the immense longing for the Lord, looking forward to the day He will come.

But beginning with Gaudete Sunday, we feel a heightened sense of joyous anticipation as we recognize that the Awaited One is now near.

"The one who has the bride is the bridegroom; the best man, who stands and listens to him, rejoices greatly at the bridegroom's voice. So this joy of mine has been made complete" (John 3: 29). Listen for His voice. The Wedding week of the Lamb will soon begin.

God wed Himself to Man through Jesus Christ. By becoming one with humanity, God paved the way for an eternal union. He freely and totally gives himself to us in hopes that we might give ourselves to Him in return.

Your marriage should mirror this gift of the Incarnation—becoming one through a sincere gift of self and establishing a fruitful, life-giving covenant between you. It seems appropriate then that this week focuses on building up your relationship as husband and wife.

By picking up this book in the first place, you and your spouse committed to growing spiritually together this Advent; however, with the busyness that surrounds this time of year, you might find your marriage has slipped on your list of priorities. So this week, give yourself permission to put first things first.

During this third week, we will focus on intentionally building up your marriage by examining the example of biblical spouses and discussing meaningful ways in which you can strengthen your relationship with your husband or wife during this season.

# Reclaiming our Identities

**Read: Genesis 3:1-19**

*Now the snake was the most cunning of all the wild animals that the LORD God had made. He asked the woman, "Did God really say, 'You shall not eat from any of the trees in the garden'?"*

*The woman answered the snake: "We may eat of the fruit of the trees in the garden;*

*it is only about the fruit of the tree in the middle of the garden that God said, 'You shall not eat it or even touch it, or else you will die.'"*

*But the snake said to the woman: "You certainly will not die!*

*God knows well that when you eat of it your eyes will be opened and you will be like gods, who know good and evil."*

*The woman saw that the tree was good for food and pleasing to the eyes, and the tree was desirable for gaining wisdom. So she took some of its fruit and ate it; and she also gave some to her husband, who was with her, and he ate it.*

*Then the eyes of both of them were opened, and they knew that they were naked; so they sewed fig leaves together and made loincloths for themselves.*

*When they heard the sound of the LORD God walking about in the garden at the breezy time of the day, the man and his wife hid themselves from the LORD God among the trees of the garden.*

*The LORD God then called to the man and asked him: Where are you?*

*He answered, "I heard you in the garden; but I was afraid, because I was naked, so I hid."*

*Then God asked: Who told you that you were naked? Have you eaten from the tree of which I had forbidden you to eat?*

*The man replied, "The woman whom you put here with me—she gave me fruit from the tree, so I ate it."*

*The LORD God then asked the woman: What is this you have done? The woman answered, "The snake tricked me, so I ate it."*

*Then the LORD God said to the snake:*

*Because you have done this,*
*cursed are you*
*among all the animals, tame or wild;*
*On your belly you shall crawl,*
*and dust you shall eat*
*all the days of your life.*

*I will put enmity between you and the woman,*

*and between your offspring and hers;*
*They will strike at your head,*

*while you strike at their heel.*

*To the woman he said:*

*I will intensify your toil in childbearing;*
*in pain you shall bring forth children.*
*Yet your urge shall be for your husband,*
*and he shall rule over you.*

*To the man he said: Because you listened to your wife and ate from*
*the tree about which I commanded you, You shall not eat from it,*

*Cursed is the ground because of you!*
*In toil you shall eat its yield*
*all the days of your life.*

*Thorns and thistles it shall bear for you,*

*and you shall eat the grass of the field.*

*By the sweat of your brow*

*you shall eat bread,*
*Until you return to the ground,*
*from which you were taken;*
*For you are dust,*
*and to dust you shall return.*

**Reflect:**

In the beginning, God made man and woman in His "image and likeness." We see this phrase later in Genesis to describe the relationship between Adam and his own son, Seth. It indicates an intimate, familial relationship between us and God, established by our very being. It denotes our identity as His children––a truth foundational for the rest of our lives, including our marriages.

In this passage from Genesis, the evil one, disguised as the serpent, convinced Eve to eat the fruit of the forbidden tree. He did this not by forcing her, and not because Eve was stupid or weak, but by bringing into question her identity as a daughter of God.

The serpent casts doubt on Eve's perception of God: instead of a loving Father who desires her good, she sees an unjust lawgiver bent on withholding gifts from her.

And as she loses the sense of who God is, she also loses the sense of who *she* is.

She begins to grasp at things "pleasing to the eyes" in an attempt to reclaim her purpose and identity. But instead, she finds loneliness and heartache.

Eve's loss of identity causes a rift in the union between God and man, and in turn between Eve and Adam. We still often feel the effects of this rift in our own relationships and in our marriages. Through sin, we broke the unity we had in Eden. We lost the perfect communion for which we were made. We spend our earthly lives trying to find our identities in other aspects of our lives, searching to fill the ache that was left behind. We enter into our marriages burdened with the weight of the sin of our first parents.

But thankfully, that wasn't the end of the story.

In the same moment that the Lord speaks of the consequences of sin, He also speaks the first promise of a redeemer, a promise we see fulfilled during this season. God in His mercy sent a savior to open, once again, the opportunity for oneness. He sent His son to not merely return us to the paradise of Adam and Eve, but to make way for an eternal marriage between God and man--so that we might never again forget who we are.

We can taste the shadow of that eternal marriage through the sanctification of our marriages on earth.

**Act:**

Discuss with your spouse the following questions: Do you have a strong sense of your identity as a son or daughter of God? In what ways does this affect your relationship with God and with each other? In what areas of your marriage do you feel the rift of sin most clearly?

As husband and wife, you have the unique ability to see one another as God sees you--recognizing, often with more clarity, His Goodness and Beauty dwelling within your beloved. Speak that truth into the heart and mind of your spouse today. Affirm your spouse's identity as a son or daughter of God, either verbally or through writing. Help one another reclaim your truest selves, and watch your marriage flourish.

# Redeeming Marriage

**Read: Matthew 1: 18-25**

*Now this is how the birth of Jesus Christ came about. When his mother Mary was betrothed to Joseph, but before they lived together, she was found with child through the holy Spirit.*

*Joseph her husband, since he was a righteous man, yet unwilling to expose her to shame, decided to divorce her quietly.*

*Such was his intention when, behold, the angel of the Lord appeared to him in a dream and said, "Joseph, son of David, do not be afraid to take Mary your wife into your home. For it is through the holy Spirit that this child has been conceived in her.*

*She will bear a son and you are to name him Jesus, because he will save his people from their sins."*

*All this took place to fulfill what the Lord had said through the prophet:*

*"Behold, the virgin shall be with child and bear a son,*

*and they shall name him Emmanuel,"*

*which means "God is with us."*

*When Joseph awoke, he did as the angel of the Lord had commanded him and took his wife into his home.*

*He had no relations with her until she bore a son, and he named him Jesus.*

**Reflect:**

Of course, you can't talk about Christian marriage (especially during Advent) without looking at the perfect example of marriage set by the Blessed Mother and her holy spouse Saint Joseph.

The Church considers Mary the new Eve because her "yes" to God undid the debt caused by the Eve's "no." Similarly, Joseph's obedience reverses the example of disobedience set by Adam. We might then consider Saint Joseph as a new Adam in anticipation of Jesus or "the last Adam" as described by Saint Paul in his letter to the Corinthians.

In the Garden, Adam doesn't protect his wife from the lies of the Evil One; instead, he stands idly by while the serpent corrupts her identity, and in turn, his own. On the other hand, Saint Joseph protects his wife (and her unborn child) from both spiritual dangers like scandal and shame, and physical ones like the threat posed by Herod. Saint Joseph defends her dignity and her identity as a daughter of God and helps Mary live out the call given to her.

The new Eve and her spouse willingly cooperated with God's grace and perfectly reflected Him through their union. The marriage of Mary and Joseph, through which comes the Awaited Savior, brought healing and new life into the marriage of our first parents and therefore, into yours.

John Paul II writes in *Redemptoris Custos*: "But whereas Adam and Eve were the source of evil which was unleashed on the world, Joseph and Mary are the summit from which holiness spreads all over the earth. The Savior began the work of salvation by this virginal and holy union, wherein is manifested his all-powerful will to purify and sanctify the family - that sanctuary of love and cradle of life."(4)

Through their humility and radical trust in the Lord, the Blessed Mother and Saint Joseph stand as an example for all couples on how to fully embrace and live out God's original plan for us.

**Act:**
Intercessory prayer is a prayer of petition that you make on behalf of another person. It makes you a conduit of grace between God and your spouse, in the same way that Mary was a conduit of grace for her husband. Her openness to God's will paved the way for Joseph to attain union with God through his own "yes."

Ask your spouse what he or she needs prayers for today. What is weighing on her heart? What is he struggling with? What virtues do you both need to live out your shared vocation? Then, bring those petitions immediately to God through prayer.

You don't need to come up with a poetic spontaneous prayer (though if you want to, go for it!). Otherwise, a simple Hail Mary or Our Father will suffice. Invite the Holy Spirit into your heart and with His guidance, this time of intercessory prayer will bring about a deeper intimacy with your beloved and a deeper union with God.

(4) Pope John Paul II, "Redemptoris Custos." *The Holy See*, 1989.

https://www.vatican.va/content/john-paul-ii/en/apost_exhortations/
documents/hf_jp-ii_exh_15081989_redemptoris-custos.html

# Trust

As you focus on preparing your marriage this week for Christ's coming, take time to contemplate the union of the Holy Spouses--Saint Joseph and Our Lady--and the stirrings of their hearts as they journeyed to meet their long-awaited child.

It makes sense that the word *trust* has origins in the Latin root word *fid*, meaning loyalty and faithfulness, when you consider that the life of the Holy Family truly embodies trust. Every part of Jesus's conception, birth, and early life testifies to Mary and Joseph's consistent surrender, knowing their lives belong to the Lord.

Consider the Annunciation, in Mary's receptivity that the Father's will "be done to me according to [His] word" (Luke 1:38)--in spite of the life-changing, world-changing herald that must have brought with it some level of surprise and apprehension. In Joseph's own visit from an angel, instructing him to keep his betrothal to Mary, without fear (Matthew 1:20).

Consider Mary and Joseph's arduous journey to Bethlehem, encompassing obedience to Caesar *and* to the will of God. Physical discomfort, a deficiency of welcome, community, or even a place to stay. Yet bearing, quite literally, an abundance of joy in the Savior's birth.

Consider their flight to Egypt, forewarned through yet another angelic message telling of Herod's intent to find and harm the infant Jesus. Abandonment to the Lord's protection; a sheltering of one another and of their precious child.

Consider the presentation of Jesus, with Simeon's words to Mary that "you yourself a sword will pierce": a prefiguring of the Cross, and a recognition of the intimate shared experiences between her heart and the heart of her son (Luke 2:35).

What common threads do these instances share, and what can we, as spouses, learn from the Holy Spouses about trust?

Observe how the major Scriptural events we know of Christ's early life were foretold to them: future plans and challenges brought to Mary and Joseph by messengers of the Lord's providence. Though we assume their good intentions, the Gospel writers don't share with us whether these messengers are interested in Mary and Joseph's reactions to their foretellings. Instead, we're left to ponder how the Holy Spouses might have reacted to the news: bearing the Word made flesh. Following through on their engagement and marriage amid worries of disgrace. Fleeing a threat to their child's life. Entering into the pain and suffering of the Crucifixion.

It seems too obvious to say that we, in our own marriages, are called to trust in the Lord even when the way forward seems marked with danger or doubt; to enter into our own pain. And it might seem like Mary and Joseph were forced into roles of passivity, simply there to hear whatever news and changes the Lord had in store. Yet they are their own agents, accepting His will and taking action with a bold, holy confidence:

*May it be done to me* (Luke 1:38).

*He...took his wife into his home* (Matthew 1:24).

*Joseph rose and took the child and his mother by night and departed for Egypt* (Matthew 2:14).

We can also become more active participants, not just recipients, of the Lord's will. Uncertainty and suffering are unavoidable, but passivity isn't.

Choosing to embrace challenges--to really feel the strain and doubt they might bring, rather than mentally pushing them aside--is a lifelong pursuit. Meditate on these moments of uncertainty and surprise that marked the begetting of Jesus and early marriage of Mary and Joseph, and look to the Holy Family's deep, abiding trust: "The home of Nazareth, wherein the earthly trinity lived its round of mutual love and obedience, was indeed different from any other home...Because it is the light, we can see our way."(5)

**Act:**
Discuss how your respective temperaments and personalities react to difficult news or times of uncertainty: do these times make you feel helpless, or inspire a desire to act? Do you resist them or try to enter in?

How can you love your spouse in his or her inclinations when it comes to trusting in the Lord, and what are practical ways to help one another increase your trust in Him?

(5) Bl. Fulton Sheen, *Three to Get Married.* Scepter Press, 1996.

# Understanding

Until today, this week's reflections have been heavily Scriptural, offering insights into preparing your marriage for the coming of Christ. What does it look like to practically prepare your marriage?

Mary and Joseph's union was marked by total trust--in the Father and in one another--and by a saintly integration of body and soul that models chaste love. In their witness, we find a reclaiming of the obedient love and spousal devotion that were present in the Garden before the fall. What are we to do when we strive to be like Joseph and Our Lady, but more often find ourselves, in our concupiscence, like Adam and Eve?

Though division and lack of understanding were a consequence of the fall, they aren't our destiny.

In this third week of Advent, we light a rose-colored candle to signify our confidence and joy: *gaudete*. Rejoice. God the Father will so soon be with us in the flesh, taking on the very human form that once caused the first break between Him and His children and offering endless mercy and hope. The embodiment of our redemption through the birth of His Son..

In what ways might He be drawing your relationship into deeper understanding this week? What practical steps can you take to grow in union and minimize division?

Deeper understanding might look like conversations about your expectations for family holiday commitments, budgeting for gifts, and for what activities, devotions, or traditions you'd like to take on for the rest of this Advent. It might look like dedicating time to pray as a couple, to plan a date night amid your busyness, or to ask your beloved how you can serve, assist, or take something off his or her plate this week.

Pursue the sacraments, as well. The graces of reconciliation, Adoration, and the Eucharist offer incredible clarity--the clearer your soul, the more visible Christ is through you.

**Act:**

During Advent, you look to the future with joy, while immersing yourself in the rich anticipation of the present. That anticipation, along with the coming end of the calendar year, is ripe for dreaming. Today, sit with your beloved and dream together!

Talk about your hopes for your marriage in the months ahead: In what areas of your relationship (emotional, spiritual, financial, home and family) do you desire to grow? What professional or hobby-related projects are you eager to take on? What future investments (home, travel, education, charitable) are you ready to start saving toward?

# Protection

Throughout this week, you've had opportunities to consider the ways in which the marriage of Mary and Joseph, sacred and holy in their trust, understanding, and obedience, redeems the fallenness of Eve and Adam. Today, consider the ways in which these virtues allow the Holy Spouses to protect one another, and how you and your beloved might abide by their example.

The Scriptures account how Joseph protects Mary's reputation and physical well-being throughout the Annunciation, journey to Bethlehem, and flight to Egypt. Unlike Adam, who stands by and attempts to absolve himself of blame, Saint Joseph is accountable and active in his desire to protect his bride and family. Together with Mary, he shelters the infant Jesus and strives to create a place of peace and safety, even amid dangerous, uncertain circumstances.

How is the Father calling you and your spouse to protect one another? How is He calling you to safeguard your marriage? During this season of heightened busyness and stress, you might feel greater temptations to complain about your beloved or to prioritize social engagements at the cost of quality time with one another. These temptations are normal, and time spent in community is good! It's worth identifying, however, the habits that nurture your relationship, and those that sap it of life.

Writer and Christian convert Sheldon Vanauken describes falling in love with his wife Davy in his memoir *A Severe Mercy*. As they grew in trust and tenderness, Sheldon and Davy expressed a desire to nurture their relationship by means of a boundary that would protect their hopes to serve one another over themselves and to let love flourish; they called it "The Shining Barrier."

What The Shining Barrier signified, he says, "was simply this question: what will be best for our love? Should one of us change a pattern of behavior that bothered the other, or should the other learn to accept? Well, which would be better for our love? Which way would be better, in any choice or decision, in the light of our single goal: to be in love as long as life might last?"(6)

Protecting your relationship and emotional intimacy allows your relationship to thrive, equipping you and your spouse to face the world hand in hand, facing outward to bear the love of Christ.

**Act:**
Consider the example of the Holy Spouses, and talk today about how you can protect your relationship from unnecessary stress, overcommitments, and gossip.

Think of ways to be a shelter for one another; a place of deepest comfort and safety for each other: How will you talk about points of disagreement with family and friends? What level of social and family commitments do you each expect and feel comfortable with this season?

How do you each feel received in moments of vulnerability, and are there specific ways you can accept one another's weaknesses more fully (through listening in a neutral way, refraining from interruptions or unsolicited advice, through offering words of apology and forgiveness, communicating in an empathetic way, and more)?

(6) Sheldon Vanauken, *A Severe Mercy*, HarperOne, 2009.

# Divine Seeing

We are in the home stretch of Advent now! Christmas is in sight, and this week in particular, you may feel yourself getting swept up into the excitement of the upcoming festivities. Allow yourself to remain in the present--the time of preparation is not yet over, with the fruits of preparation still to be revealed.

To close out this third week, let's slow down and take time to pray with a form of prayer called *Visio Divina*.

The Church has always considered sacred art to hold a necessary role in the spiritual life of the faithful. One document from the Council of Trent "On the Invocation, Veneration, Relics of Saints, and Sacred Images" speaks of their importance:

...great profit is derived from all sacred images, not only because the people are thereby admonished of the benefits and gifts bestowed upon them by Christ, but also because the miracles which God has performed by means of the saints, and their salutary examples, are set before the eyes of the faithful; so that they may give God thanks for those things, may order their own lives and manners in imitation of the saints, and may be excited to adore and love God, and to cultivate piety.(7)

*Visio Divina*, or "Divine Seeing," uses beauty (in the form of art) to facilitate an encounter with the Divine. Don't worry! Prior knowledge of art history isn't required to meet God in this form of prayer.

The steps for *Visio Divina* are similar to the steps you followed when praying *Lectio Divina* during the first week and easy to follow. This practice will help you become more aware of the Lord's presence in your life and can even work well when combined with other meditative forms of prayer like *Lectio,* or even the Rosary.

You can find suggestions for other works of art to use for further mediation in the Appendix.

*The Dream of Joseph, Rembrandt*

## HOW TO PRAY VISIO DIVINA

1. Begin by identifying the piece you will use during this time of prayer. You could use a traditional or contemporary piece of religious art or even an icon. Today we will pray with a painting of *The Dream of Joseph*, by the prolific Dutch artist Rembrandt. (For the Scriptural passage that serves as Rembrandt's inspiration, see Matthew 2: 13-15).

   Get in a comfortable position and breathe deeply, stilling your mind and opening your heart.

2. Gaze at the image. Notice the colors used, the lighting, the details in the foreground and background. What do you feel as you look at it? What draws your attention?

3. Spend time meditating on whatever aspect of the image strikes you the most. How is God speaking to you through this image? Why do you think God drew your attention to this particular part? Does it relate to your prayer from this week's focus?

4. Spend time to rest in silence and dwell in the presence of God. Allow what has been stirred up in your souls during the previous steps to take root.

5. Discuss your prayer with your spouse and create an action plan based on your conversation with God. What is the next step in this area of your life? What practical resolutions can you commit to, and how can you incorporate your prayer into your life?

(7)   Twenty-Fifth   Session   of   the   Council   of   Trent.

https://www.ewtn.com/catholicism/library/twentyfifth-session-of-the-council-of-trent-1492

# Week 4: Preparing Your Hearts

## FOURTH SUNDAY OF ADVENT

We are now just days away from Christmas morning; our time of preparation is almost complete. You and your spouse have walked through different areas of your shared life, going deeper each day and readying yourself for the coming of Christ.

This week, you will shift from an active preparation to a more contemplative one, in an imitation of our Blessed Mother who kept the mysteries of the Incarnation and pondered them in her heart (Luke 2:19).

In these final days before Christmas, as the busyness of the season reaches its peak, we invite you into stillness by delving deeper into prayer, opening your heart wider and giving Christ permission to fill it with Himself. This time of contemplation does not need to be extravagant; rather, in imitation of the first Christmas, make your prayer a simple and sincere gift of self to Our Lord.

On the next page you will find a Litany of Advent to pray daily until Christmas Eve. We hope this simple prayer will draw you closer to His

Sacred Heart and to one another as you come to the end of this Advent season.

You may choose to pray this Litany once, or several times a day. You may find a certain line that strikes you differently each time you read it or hear the Holy Spirit calling you to reflect on it throughout the day.

There is no "right way" to use this prayer. Let Him guide you through these final days to where He wants to meet you on Christmas morning.

The Awaited Savior is almost here. Come, let us finally prepare ourselves to adore Him.

*Turn the page for the Litany.*

# A Litany for Advent

A litany is a prayer consisting of repeated invocations, intended to invite those praying into contemplation of the different facets of a single idea--titles of Jesus or Mary, like the Litany of Loreto; pursuits of a virtue, like the Litany of Humility, or the intercession of of holy men and women from throughout the centuries, like the Litany of the Saints.

The more frequently you think about something desirable, the more you desire it and the more gravity it takes on in your mind. Jesus comes to us this very week, in the purity of a newborn child, to enter the deepest desire of all: our human hearts' ache for intimacy and understanding. He meets us, and redeems us, in the ache.

We wrote this Litany for Advent to turn your gaze to His coming: on the nearness of His birth, on the Incarnation, and on Mary and Joseph's roles as spouses in the Nativity story. Since this fourth week of Advent varies in length from year to year, pray the litany daily from the Fourth Sunday of Advent through Christmas Eve, meditating on the resonance of Jesus's birth, and asking the Lord to let the hope of his coming take root and flourish in your relationships.

**Let us Pray:**

Heavenly Father, your love took on human flesh and descended to us through the birth of Christ, your Son. May your love take root in us these Advent and Christmas seasons, and all the days of our life.

Love incarnate, inspire our hope.
Love revealed, bring us fully alive.
Love made flesh, make of us a gift.
Love embodied, draw us close to you.

*Response: Be born in us.*
Jesus, the Christ child, *be born in us.*
Jesus, Emmanuel,
Jesus, true God and true man,
Jesus, fruit of Mary,

*Response: We pray.*
That the hiddenness of your humble birth abide in the hidden parts of our hearts, *we pray.*
That the hope of your birth light an inexhaustible flame and sustain us always,
That the doors of heaven, opened by your birth, beckon us to your eternal wedding feast,
That the profound reality of your birth restore and enliven us,

Lord Jesus, dwell in us.
Mother Mary, shelter us in your womb.
Saint Joseph, protect and harbor us.
Holy Family, pray for us.

Amen.

# The Incarnation: What We've Been Awaiting All Along

It's hard *not* to think of anticipation during Advent: the lists, the shopping, the careful, intentional gift wrapping and preparations. Now, on Christmas Eve, there's a sense of bated breath. Even as you finish up last-minute shopping or making your holiday meal, take a moment for quiet today to feel the anticipation.

The Earth pauses on the brink of transformation; the understanding that His coming means nothing will ever be the same. When you exhale, will the words *glory* and *alleluia* fall from your lips?

We've awaited Christ's birth through the past several weeks. His coming is the ultimate gift of self: an *embodiment* and enfleshment of divine love, freely given. A body that will seek comfort and nourishment from the body of His mother; a body that will grow, travel, preach. A body that will ultimately be broken, bloodied, and poured out.

The birth of Jesus is humble. Poor. Hidden. He comes among us as someone so little, simply as He is.

Consider the intensity of love in the gaze between two deeply bonded persons. What depths of emotion Mary must have experienced as she looked into the face of her newborn child, and with what wonder Jesus must have regarded the face of His mother.

What do you feel and experience when you gaze upon your beloved? In the same humility, poverty, and simplicity, can you come before one another, trusting you'll be looked upon with complete acceptance and tenderness? Can you be Christ's hands and feet to each other, serving with love in all things?

On this vigil of Christmas, He is here. He dwells with us, and abides with us, from this first night to his last breath and for all eternity.

Among us at last, He is "the realization of what is hoped for and evidence of things not seen" (Hebrews 11:1).

*We hope the reflections and prayers found here bring something new to your spiritual life throughout the year. See the appendix that follows for additional Scripture and art resourced to enrich your prayer throughout the Christmas season.*

# Appendix

Consider the modes of prayer introduced in this book. If you've enjoyed praying with *Lectio Divina* or Ignatian Meditation, you might find it fruitful to meditate on the Incarnation and Christ, the Awaited One's, arrival in the language of Christmas hymns. Try the following to get started:

*Word of the Father*
*Now in flesh appearing*
*O come, let us adore Him*
-From "O Come All Ye Faithful"

*Veiled in flesh*
*The Godhead see,*
*Hail the Incarnate deity*
-From "Hark, the Herald Angels Sing"

*Suddenly the Lord descending*
*In his temple shall appear*
-From "Angels From the Realms of Glory"

*Radiant beams from thy holy face,*
*With the dawn of redeeming grace,*
*Jesus, Lord at thy birth.*
-From "Silent Night"

# Further Scripture Resources

Deepen your relationship with the Word of God, Jesus Christ this Christmas. Use *Lectio Divina* or Ignatian Mediation to pray with the following Scripture passages.

**For *Lectio Divina***
Isaiah 2:1-5
Isaiah 9:1-6
Isaiah 52:7-10
Isaiah 60:1-6
Isaiah 62:1-5
Isaiah 62:11-12
Isaiah 63:15-19; 64:2-7
Jeremiah 31:7-14

Luke 1:46-56
Luke 1:67-80
Luke 2:41-52
Luke 3:21-22
John 1:35-51

Romans 13:11-14
Ephesians 1:3-14
Titus 3:4-7

## For Ignatian Meditation

Matthew 2:1-12

Matthew 2:13-18

Matthew 3:13-17

Luke 1: 39-56

Luke 2:4-20

Luke 2:22-38

# Further Visio Divina Resources

Encounter the long-awaited Christ through beauty this Christmas. Below you will find a list of religious art for you to meditate on during this season.

*The Annunciation* by Fra Angelico

*The Annunciation* by Henry Ossawa Tanner

*Mary and Joseph on the Way to Bethlehem* by Hugo van der Goes

*The Census at Bethlehem* by Peter Bruegel the Elder

*Saint Joseph Seeks Lodging in Bethlehem* by James Tissot

*The Nativity* by Arthur Hughes

*The Nativity of the Lord* by Michael Corsini

*A Quiet Moment* by Timothy Schmalz

*Adoration of the Christ Child* by Gerard van Honthorst

*The Adoration of the Shepherds* by El Greco

*The Adoration of the Shepherds* by Caravaggio

*Adoration of the Magi* by Botticelli

*Madonna and Child Painting* by Giovanni Battista Salvi Il Sassoferrato

*The Flight into Egypt* by Adam Elsheimer

*The Flight into Egypt* by Blair Piras

*Rest on the Flight to Egypt* by Orazio Gentileschi

*Presentation in the Temple* by Rembrandt

# About the Authors

CARISSA PLUTA, AUTHOR

Carissa Pluta is a blogger, freelance writer, and the Associate Editor for Spoken Bride who has a seemingly insatiable desire to create and cultivate beauty in the world. Carissa is a regular contributor for Radiant Magazine, and her writing has also been featured on Aleteia, Grotto Network, and Blessed is She, among other publications. Carissa lives outside of Philadelphia with her husband (a FOCUS parish missionary) and their two children. Learn more about her at her blog themythretold.com or follow her on Instagram @carissa_pluta.

STEPHANIE CALIS, AUTHOR

Stephanie is a founder of Spoken Bride and author of the book *Invited: The Ultimate Catholic Wedding Planner* (Pauline, 2016 & 2021), a #1 Amazon bestseller in Weddings. An advocate for the power of beauty and of authentic relationship to draw hearts to the Church, she has been featured on EWTN's *At Home with Jim and Joy*, in *Family Foundations* Magazine, and on Brides.com, Blessed Is She, and The Young-CatholicWoman. Stephanie and her husband live in Maryland with their four children.

ANDI COMPTON, DESIGNER

Combining years of professional event coordination, calligraphy, graphic design, and art with a passion for helping couples truly enter into the sacrament of marriage, Andi founded Spoken Bride in 2016 with Stephanie Calis and Jiza Zito. She and her husband received a nuptial blessing from Pope Emeritus Benedict XVI on their honeymoon in 2007, and are the parents of five rambunctious children. They live, work, and play in San Diego, California.

# About the Publisher

Have you fallen in love? This community is for you. But it's not just any love we're talking about.

> The Spoken Bride is a romantic--alight with anticipation for her wedding day, but she knows the foremost romance in life is a divine one. It shapes her entire identity: she knows she is worthy, beautiful, dignified, simply because she is.

She is a fiancée, best friend, sister, bride, and helpmate to heaven. Beauty pierces her heart and draws her into the sacred. She wants not only her wedding, but her marriage to reflect this in every way: through awe-inspiring liturgy, decor, and photographs, each infused, above all, with the radiant beauty only made manifest in sincere holiness. No matter her past, she has a love for all that is pure. She desires nothing more or less than to make a complete gift of herself. She chases fearlessly after virtue, knowing excellence is the path to true freedom, and freedom is for love.

> Deeply, profoundly, she is in love.

We're here to spark something. To showcase wedding inspiration that fixes our eyes on the beauty of the Creator. To offer a resource for finding vendors who not only have a wealth of talent for their craft, but who are on fire for the sacrament of marriage. To help you plan for the biggest day of your life, but also for a lifetime: a marriage free, faithful, total, and fruitful in every sense. To be a witness, galvanizing the culture with the goodness, truth, and beauty of Catholic marriage. We're here for you, in community and sisterhood, and we are ultimately here to walk alongside you in living out authentic love between man and wife. The kind of love that makes people stop and take notice. The kind that's set apart because it transcends this world.

Join us at www.spokenbride.com for inspiration from real Catholic weddings, wisdom from brides and newlyweds, a Catholic wedding vendor guide, and a shop featuring Catholic wedding programs and much more.